Writer's Notebook

By the Editors of TIME For Kids

Teacher Created Materials
PUBLISHING

TCM 10146 (iz65)

**TIME For Kids• Writer's Notebook
Level A**
Copyright © 2006
Time Inc.

TIME For Kids and the Red Border Design are
registered trademarks of Time Inc. All rights reserved.
Developed in collaboration with *Exploring Writing* and
distributed by Teacher Created Materials Publishing.

TIME For Kids
Editorial Director: Keith Garton
Editor: Jonathan Rosenbloom
Project Editor: The Quarasan Group, Inc.
Design Production: The Quarasan Group, Inc.
Illustrator: The Quarasan Group, Inc.
Teacher Reviewers: Holly Albrecht, WI; Paula
Barr, KS; Renae Brooks, IL; Dee Elliott, GA;
Susan Geddes, TX; Martha Jean, CA; Ryann
Kelso, IL; Joan Ray, FL; Stephanie Schiada,
OR; Laura Shepherd, OK; Sherie Willis, NV

Exploring Writing™
Copyright © 2006
Teacher Created Materials Publishing

Teacher Created Materials Publishing
Publisher: Rachelle Cracchiolo, M.S. Ed.
Editor-in-Chief: Sharon Coan, M.S. Ed.
Editorial Project Manager: Dona Herweck Rice

ISBN: 0-7439-0146-0

Teacher Created
Materials Publishing
5301 Oceanus Drive
Huntington Beach, CA 92649
www.tcmpub.com

Illustration credits:
Page 5: (b) Ken Bowser; p.7: Mike Werner; p.8: (tr) Ken Bowser; p.9: (tr) Ken Bowser; p.10: Ken Bowser;
p.11: Ken Bowser; p.12: (tr) Ken Bowser; p.13: Ken Bowser; p.14: (tr) Mike Werner; p.20–21: Ken Bowser; p.23:
Ken Bowser; p.24: (m) Ken Bowser; p.25: Tim Foley; p.26: Mike Werner; p.27: Mike Werner; p.28: (br) Tim Foley;
p.32: (tr) Tim Foley; p.38: (mr) Tim Foley; p.40: Tim Foley; p.45: Tim Foley; p.47: Ken Bowser; p.48: Ken Bowser;
p.49: (t) Ken Bowser; p.50: Tim Foley; p.51: Tim Foley; p.55: Ken Bowser; p.58: (r) Tim Foley; p.59: (tr) Tim Foley;
p.60: Mike Werner; p.61: Ken Bowser; p.62: (t) Mike Werner; p.63: Mike Werner; p.64: Mike Werner; p.65: Ken
Bowser; p.68: (tr) (mr) Tim Foley

Photography credits:
Page 5: (t) PhotoDisc, Inc.; p.6: (t) PhotoDisc, Inc.; p.19: (t) PhotoDisc, Inc.; p.27: (b) PhotoDisc, Inc.; p.33:
(b) Corel Co.; p.44: (b) MetaTools Inc.; p.51: (b) PhotoDisc, Inc.; p.52: (b) PhotoDisc, Inc.; p.57: (b) Digital Stock
Corp.; p.69: (b) Artville; p.72: (r) MetaTools Inc.; p.72: (frame) Corbis, (l) Corbis, (r) Corbis, p.76: (l) PhotoDisc,
Inc., (r) PhotoDisc, Inc.

 For more writing practice: www.timeforkids.com/hh/writeideas

Table of Contents

Getting Started • Write Anywhere, Anytime • Be a List Maker • Choose a Topic • Draw Pictures

Write a First Draft • Use Your Senses

What Is Nonfiction?

What Is Fiction? • Parts of a Story

What Is a Poem?

Using Your Writer's Notebook

You can be a writer.
Write about something you know.
Tell what happened to you.
Make up a story.

Use this book to help you.
- Think about what to say.
- Write good sentences.
- Discover new words.

Get ready! Get set! Write!

Time to Write: The Way to Write

Steps For Good Writing

1 **Prewriting**—Think and plan.

My Pet Cat
black
soft
likes to play

2 **Drafting**—Write and draw.

I have a pet cat named midnight.

Her fur is soft and blak. Midnight

likes to play

4 **Revising**—Make your writing better.

> **My Pet**
>
> I have a cute pet cat named
> midnight. Her fur is soft and coal
> blak. Midnight likes to play

5 **Editing**—Fix your mistakes.

> **My Pet**
>
> I have a cute pet cat named
> midnight. Her fur is soft and coal
> blak. Midnight likes to play

6 **Publishing**—Share your writing.

> **My Pet**
>
> I have a cute pet cat named Midnight.
> Her fur is soft and coal black. Midnight
> likes to play.

Let's take a closer look at
the steps for good writing.

Prewriting

Think about what you will write. Make a plan.

Ask some questions.
Write and draw some ideas.

My Pet Cat

black

soft

likes to play

Drafting

Use your plan.

Write your ideas in sentences. Draw pictures, too.

Don't worry about mistakes. You can fix them later.

I have a pet cat named midnight.

Her fur is soft and blak. Midnight

likes to play

Revising

Read your story out loud.
Ask a friend to listen.
Does your story make sense?
Can you add better words?
Do you like what you wrote?

Look for changes in the story about Midnight.

My Pet

I have a cute pet cat named

midnight. Her fur is soft and coal

blak. Midnight likes to play

Editing and Proofreading

Read your story again.

Look for mistakes.
Fix the ones you find.

Did I write whole sentences?

Did I spell the words right?

Did I use capital letters and periods?

My Pet

I have a cute pet cat named

midnight. Her fur is soft and coal

blak. Midnight likes to play

Publishing

Share your best writing with others.
* Read your story to the class.
* Write a letter.
* Make a big book or a poster.

My Pet

I have a cute pet cat named Midnight.

Her fur is soft and coal black. Midnight

likes to play.

Getting Started

Decide what you will write about.

Look around. What do you see? What is happening?
- Write about things you know.
- Write about things you like—
a friend, a pet, a favorite game.

Try This!

Use your notebook.
Write down your ideas.

Animals I Know About

1. dogs   4. _____

2. spiders   5. _____

3. my parakeet   6. _____

Things I Like

1. my computer game

2. my rock collection

3. _____

4. _____

5. _____

My Family

1. my baby brother

2. my mom

3. _____

4. _____

5. _____

Things I'm Good At

1. riding my bike

2. drawing pictures

3. _____

4. _____

5. _____

Write Anywhere, Anytime

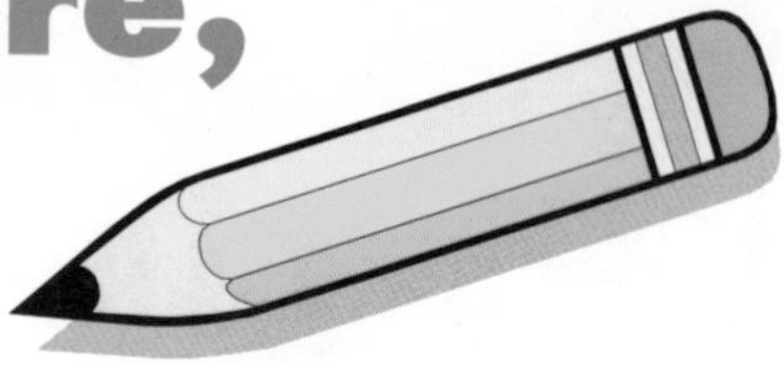

Good writers look and listen. They write down their ideas.

Try This!

Read the sentences below. Then tell about something you saw or heard.

1. I saw a hundred ants eat some bread.

2. I heard a loud fire engine last night.

3. _____

4. _____

5. _____

Good writers collect words they like.

1. love

2. snowball

3. purple

4. _____

5. _____

6. _____

Good writers make notes.

Baby Harry started walking.

Good writers keep a journal.

Tuesday

Today I went to the store with my mom. We bought new shoes. They light up.

17

Be a List Maker

Good writers make lists. They look at their lists when they need an idea for writing. Add your own words to each list.

Places I've Been

1. the beach

2. the mall

3. _____

4. _____

My Favorite Foods

1. chicken

2. cheese sandwich

3. _____

4. _____

Try This!

Here are more lists. Add words to finish each one.

My Best Animals

1. dogs

2. hamsters

3. _____

4. _____

Things I Want to Learn About

1. stars and space

2. bugs

3. _____

4. _____

Choose a Topic

A **topic** is what you write about.

Choose a topic before you start writing.
- Look at the lists you made.
- Think about who will read your story.
- Pick a topic that is interesting to you.

Ask questions to help you choose a topic.

Did I go someplace special?

Did someone I know do something brave?

Did something funny happen?

Have I read a really good book?

Try This!

Write some ideas for story topics. Then choose one to write about.

_____

_____

_____

_____

Make a Plan

You can use a web to plan your writing.
Think about your topic.
Write the topic in the middle.
List your ideas around the topic.

Sleeping in a tent

Eating outdoors

Our Camping Trip

Swimming in the lake

Hiking through the woods

2

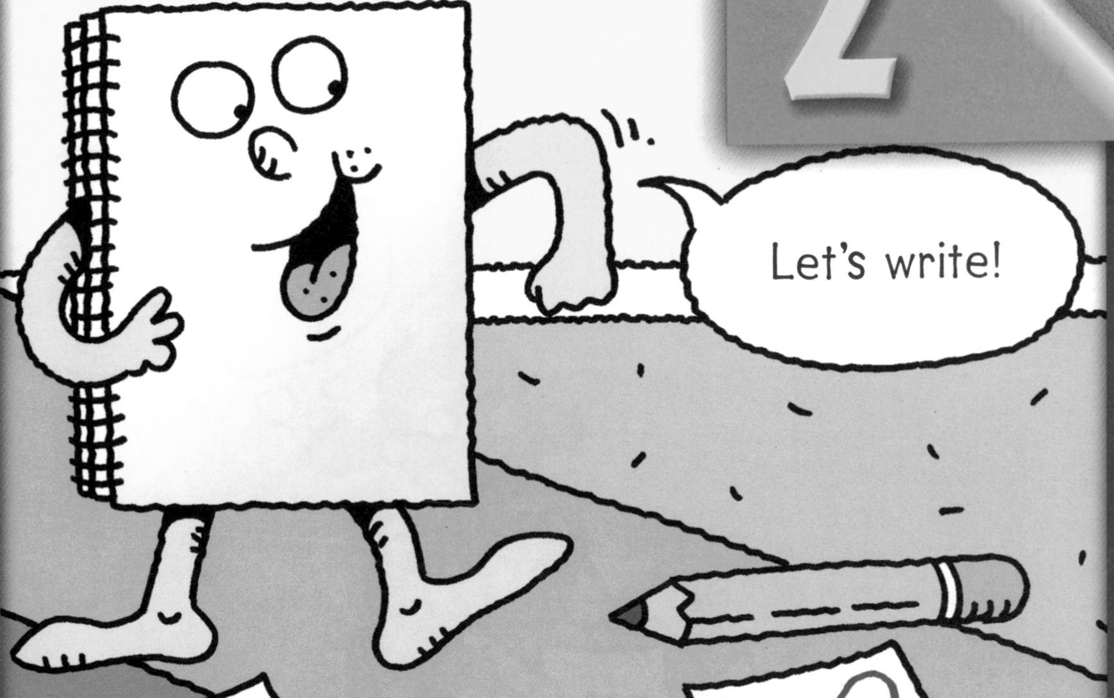

Drafting

Write a First Draft

A first draft is your first try at writing a story. Here is what to do.

- Write and draw about your topic.
- Use your word lists.
- Leave room to add words later.
- Don't worry about mistakes.
- Don't worry about spelling.

> I write my ideas in complete sentences.

TFK Tips for Writers

Just start writing. Get your ideas down on paper. You can make changes later.

A Good Start

Here is a first draft. It tells about a special dog.

There are some mistakes. The writer will fix them later.

The Wonder Dog

There was a dog named tinker. he was

a special dog. everything one color. In my

yard he made the grass blu. I did not like

blu grass so i made it green again

25

Use Your Senses

Writers tell about people, places, and things. They use sense words to tell how things look, sound, taste, smell, and feel.

Looks

muddy bright scary
pretty happy

Tastes

yummy sweet spicy
sour crunchy

Feels

hard cold bumpy
rough hot

Sounds

buzzing
loud
shrill
ringing
crying

Smells

smoky
sweet
funny
strong
clean

Time to Write

Write your own describing words here.

1. a _____ dress

2. a _____ kitten

3. a _____ story

4. a _____ car

What Is Nonfiction?

Nonfiction writing tells about something that is true or real.

A true story about yourself or another person is called **narrative nonfiction.**

Personal Narrative

A story you write about yourself is a personal narrative.

Here are some ways to get started.

- Think about a place you like to go. Tell about it.
- Recall something you did. How did you feel?
- Remember a special day. Tell what happened.

Try This!

Read this story. The writer tells about a special present.
How can you tell this story is nonfiction?

My Bike

I got a bike for my birthday.

It is red and shiny.

At first I fell down a lot.

Now I can go fast.

TFK Tips for Writers

Follow these steps when you write a personal narrative.
- Pretend you are talking to a friend.
- Tell what happened.
- Put your sentences in order.

Biography

A **biography** is a story about a real person. It tells what that person said and did. The writer shows why the person is special.

A biography gives **facts** about a person. Use these questions to help you write.

Who is my story about?

What did this person do?

When did he or she live?

Where does the story take place?

Why do we remember this person?

Try This!

Read the biography below. Which questions from page 30 does the writer use to tell you about his mother?

My Mom

My mom is a nurse. Every day she goes to the hospital. She takes care of sick people. She helps them get better.

Report

A **report** gives facts about a certain subject.

When you write a report,
choose an interesting subject.

Look and listen.
Read to find out more.

Use words and pictures
to tell what you learned.

TFK Tips for Writers

Ask your teacher to help you find books about
your subject.

Try This!

Read the report below. What facts does the writer want you to know?

Shells

A snail lives in a shell.

A turtle has a shell.

A peanut grows inside a shell.

A baby bird comes from a shell.

TFK Tips for Writers

You can write a good report.
- Pick a subject you like and want to know about.
- Give your report a title.
- Write the most important things you learn about your subject.
- Be sure everything is true and not made up.
- Add pictures to go with your writing.

Friendly Letter

You can send a message to
a friend who lives far away.
You can also write to a friend nearby.
This kind of writing is called a **friendly letter.**

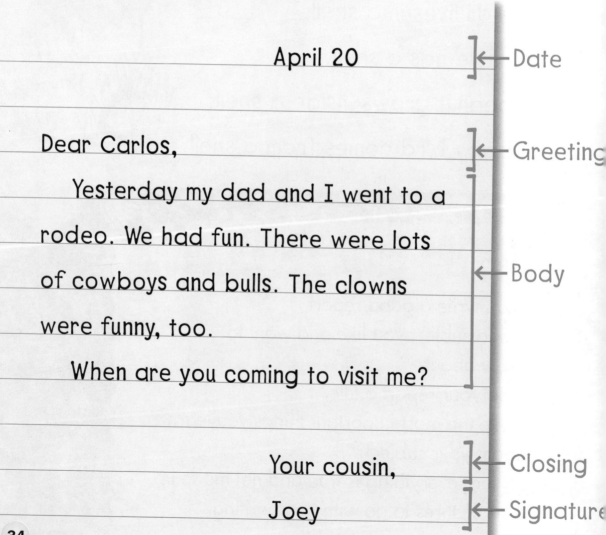

April 20 ←— Date

Dear Carlos, ←— Greeting

    Yesterday my dad and I went to a
rodeo. We had fun. There were lots
of cowboys and bulls. The clowns
were funny, too.

    When are you coming to visit me? ←— Body

Your cousin, ←— Closing

Joey ←— Signature

Address an Envelope

Send your letter in an envelope. Write your friend's address in the middle. Put your address in the upper left-hand corner. Put a stamp in the upper right-hand corner.

Joey Martinez
115 Mountain View
Tucson, AZ 85700

Carlos Rivera
358 Green Street
Denver, CO 80200

TFK Tips for Writers

Write a letter to share news with a friend.
- Use the special form for a letter.
- Tell about what you are doing.
- Ask questions so your friend will write back.

Write About a Book

Think about a good book you have read. Why did you like it?
- Was the story funny?
- Did something exciting happen?
- Did the writer use colorful words?
- Did you learn something new?

The Doorbell Rang

by Pat Hutchins

I think this book is funny. A mother bakes cookies. Everybody keeps ringing the doorbell because they want cookies, too. You should read it to find out if there are enough cookies.

Try This!

Write the title of a book you enjoy.
Draw a picture to show what happened.
Share your work with a friend.

_____

TFK Tips for Writers

- Don't tell everything that happens! Pick out one important thing.
- Tell what you liked about the book.
- Don't tell how the story ends. Make it a surprise.

Time To Write Fiction

What Is Fiction?

A made-up story is called narrative **fiction.** This kind of story tells about things that did not really happen.

Try This!

Think about these stories. Are they fiction or real?

- A pig gets a job.
- My family takes a trip to the city.
- Two friends visit a place where people are only five inches tall.

TFK Tips for Writers

When you write fiction, tell a make-believe story. Use your imagination.

Folk tales and **fairy tales** are fiction. These stories took place long ago.

The characters are make-believe. The main character could be a giant or a dragon.

The story action is also make-believe. Sometimes animals talk and wear clothes.

Time to Write

Finish each title. Write the names of make-believe story characters. Can you tell one of these stories to your classmates?

1. The Three Little _____.

2. Goldilocks and the Three _____.

3. The Shoemaker and the _____

4. The Three Billy _____ Gruff

Parts of a Story

The **setting** tells where the story takes place.

There was a little cottage deep in the woods.

The **characters** are the people or animals the story is about.

Goldilocks was a sweet little girl who liked to take walks.

The **plot** tells what happens in the story.

While the bears were away, Goldilocks went into their cottage.

Try This!

Create a character for your next story.
What does your character look like?
What does he or she do?

- Draw a picture
- Write 2 or 3 sentences describing your character.

TFK Tips for Fiction Writers

- Use your imagination.
- Tell the story in order.
- Draw pictures.

Find the Story Parts

Do you remember the story about the magic dog on page 25? Look for the setting, the characters, and the plot in the story.

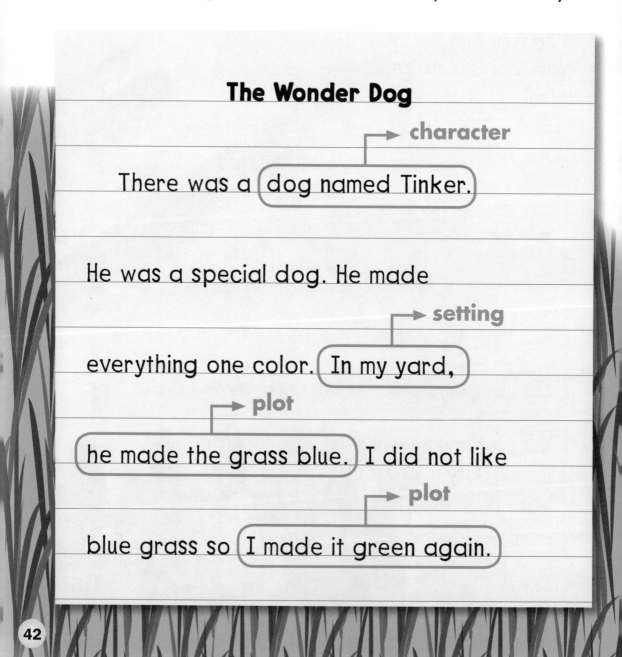

The Wonder Dog

character

There was a (dog named Tinker.)

He was a special dog. He made

setting

everything one color. (In my yard,

plot

(he made the grass blue.) I did not like

plot

blue grass so (I made it green again.)

Time to Write

Look at a story you are writing.
Be sure it has all the story parts.
Add the ones that are missing.

TFK Story Checklist

_____ My story has a main character.

_____ My story tells where the action happens.

_____ My story tells what the character does.

_____ My story tells how the character feels.

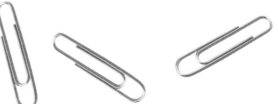

What Is a Poem?

A **poem** is a special kind of writing.
It helps you picture an idea.

A poem is like a song. It has a certain **rhythm** or **beat.**
Poems often use **rhyming** words.

Clap as you chant.

Humpty Dumpty sat on a **wall.**

Humpty Dumpty had a great **fall.**

All the king's horses

And all the king's **men,**

Couldn't put Humpty together **again.**

Fun with Words

Poems make pictures with words.

**a croaking frog
on a bumpy log**

**sandy fun in
the summer sun**

Try This!

Think of some words that paint pictures.

1. a fluffy puppy

2. a bright red fire truck

3. _____

4. _____

5. _____

Words that Rhyme

Read the pairs of words that rhyme. Add one rhyming word to each pair.

cat – mat   _____   sun – fun   _____

log – frog   _____   spill – will   _____

pig – jig   _____   get – pet   _____

pan – man   _____   sail – pail   _____

Time to Write

Use some words from the list. Make funny rhymes like these.

A big fat cat   A silly green frog
Went to town in a hat.   Sat on a log.

_____

_____

Revising

Make Your Writing Better

Good writers think about their writing.
They try to make it better.
Read your writing to a friend.
Ask some questions.

Are the sentences in order?

Will others understand?

Did I use the best words?

Does my writing make sense?

ABC

Choose a Better Title

An interesting title draws attention.

Try This!

Read the titles. Which book would you rather read? Why do you think so?

Tell Your Story in Order

Stories have a **beginning,** a **middle,** and an **end.**

Think about the story *The Three Pigs.*

Beginning	The three pigs left home.
Middle	Each pig built a house. A wolf tried to catch the pigs. He blew down two of the houses. He could not blow down the last house. He tried to get inside.
End	The wolf fell down the chimney. The pigs were safe.

Use Order Words

Good writers tell what happened. They tell the story in order.

First, Goldilocks tasted the porridge.

Next, she sat in all the chairs.

Last, she tried out the beds.

First, next, and *last* are order words. They show how the action happened.

Try This!

Write 1, 2, and 3 to tell the order. Use the order words to help you. Then read the sentences in the order that they happened.

_____ Next, get two cookies.

_____ Last, eat it all up.

_____ First, pour some milk in a glass.

Choose Better Words

Read your story. Add words that say just what you mean.

Naming Words

A **noun** names a person, place, or thing.

Jamie wants to buy **apples.**
Jamie asked her mother for **money.**

A **pronoun** takes the place of a noun.

Jamie wants to buy apples.	**She** asked her mother for money to buy **them.**

Describing Words

An **adjective** describes, or tells about, a noun.

> **Little** Jamie wanted to buy **sweet, crunchy** apples.

Adjectives make your writing interesting. They tell how something looks, sounds, tastes, smells, or feels.

Try This!

Add an **adjective** to tell about each **noun.**

_____ train   _____ toy

_____ puppy   _____ lunch

_____ baby   _____ flower

Action Words

A **verb** is an action word. Strong verbs will help readers picture what is happening.

The ducks splash
in the pond.

Dad tells funny stories.

Mom and I bake
peanut butter cookies.

Jan and Sam laugh
at my jokes.

We visit Grandma
every Sunday.

Bunnies hide in
the tall grass.

Time to Revise

Write strong, colorful verbs that tell how these animals move.

snakes _____   monkeys _____

bunnies _____   horses _____

Sentences

A **sentence** is a group of words that tells a complete thought.

Every sentence has a **naming part** and a **doing part.**

Naming Part	Doing Part
A brown bunny	hops in the garden.

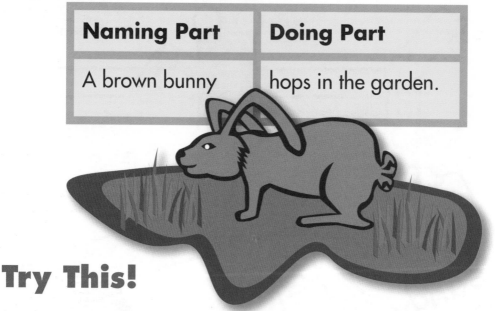

Try This!

The groups of words below are not whole sentences. Add a naming part or a doing part to finish each sentence.

1. _____ swims in the lake.

2. The big brown bear _____.

Kinds of Sentences

Good writers use different kinds of sentences.

A **telling sentence** tells something. It ends with a period.	Dan found a penny. 
An **asking sentence** asks a question. It ends with a question mark.	Did you have fun at the park? 
An **exclamatory sentence** shows strong feeling. It ends with an exclamation mark.	This soup is too hot! 

Try This!

Read each sentence. Add the right end mark.

1. I see big black clouds___   2. Do you hear thunder___

Capital Letters

Good writers use capital letters to write certain words.

the first word in a sentence	My bother plays the drums.
names of people	Carlos, Emma, Grandpa, Mrs. Benson
names of special places	Chicago, Mexico, Central Park
names of days, months, and holidays	Monday, June, Thanksgiving

Time to Edit

Read a story you have written. Check to be sure that you have used capital letters and end marks in the right places.

Spelling

Check your spelling. Good spelling helps readers understand what you write.

Listen to the sounds of words. Think about word families. Notice how some words have almost the same spelling. Add a word of your own.

bat, cat, mat, _____

pin, tin, win, _____

hop, pop, stop, _____

game, same, blame, _____

boat, coat, goat, _____

TFK Tips for Writers

- Think about words you know.
- Use a dictionary to check words you don't know.

Proofreading

When you finish writing, **proofread** your work.
Look for mistakes and fix them.
Use these marks to show what will change.

Make a capital letter.	≡	april
Add a period.	⊙	Dogs bark
Add a letter or word.	∧	tiny ant
Take out a word.	—	He was on ~~to~~ time.

Try This!

Read the story below. Look at the proofreading marks.
What changes would you make?

My Hamster Penny

My hamster is named Penny. she has soft tan
fur. She likes to ~~to~~ run on her wheel.

60

What To Publish

You **publish** your writing when you share it with others.

Choose your best work. Ask questions to help you decide.

Is my writing clear?

Will others be interested?

Did I use good words?

The Missing Tooth

I pulled out my tooth all by myself. I saved it in a lunch bag. When I got home it was missing. Where did my tooth go?

First Prize

How To Publish

You can present your writing in many ways. Try some of these.

Write and Draw a Story

Use a Computer to Make a Report

Make a Class Book

Read Your Story to Others

What do **you** want to publish? How will you do it?

Words To Know

Use lots of different words when you write. Pick the best words to say what you mean.

Try some of the words on the following pages. Add new words that you learn. Write them in your word bank.

Words Writers Often Use

and	are	can	in	my	play
am	but	I	make	not	run

Word Bank

I like to run and play.

Hard-To-Spell Words

about	talk
because	favorite
friend	here
they	said
any	

favorite ice cream

best friend

Word Bank

Rhyming Words

cat pat

pin win

cup pup

big pig

spill hill

cake bake

sing ring

duck truck

a duck on a truck

a spill on a hill

Word Bank

Color Words

red

blue

yellow

green

orange

purple

pink

brown

black

white

Word Bank

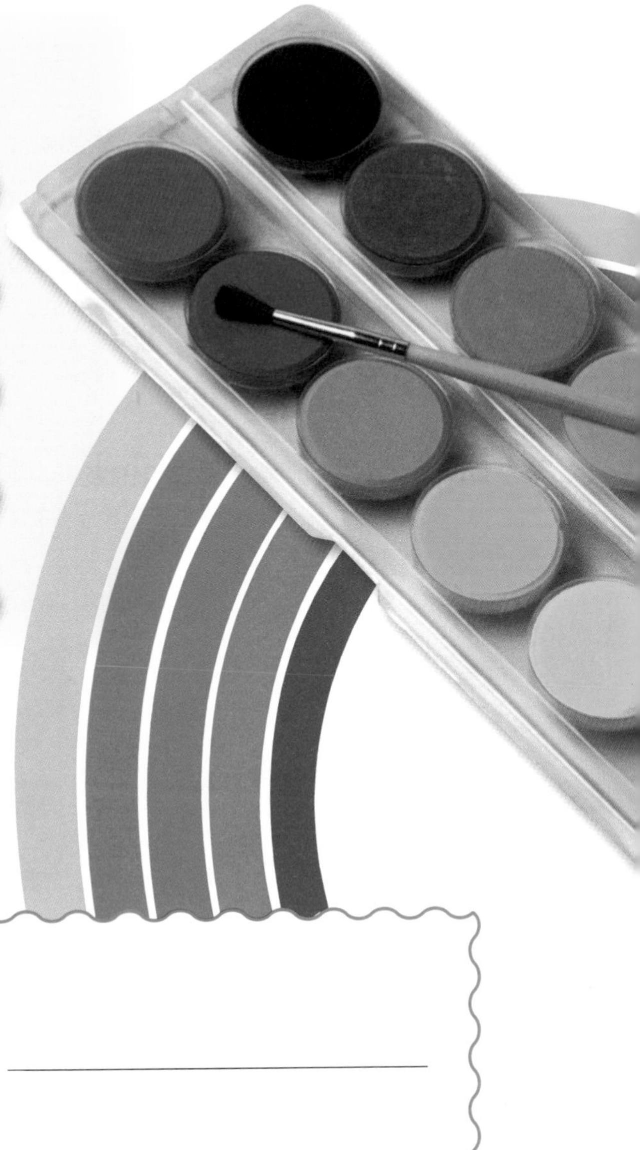

Number Words

one	1	six	6
two	2	seven	7
three	3	eight	8
four	4	nine	9
five	5	ten	10

Calendar Words

Days

Sunday	Monday	Tuesday
Wednesday	Thursday	Friday
Saturday		

Months

January	February	March
April	May	June
July	August	September
October	November	December

Family Words

father   grandpa

mother   uncle

brother   aunt

sister   cousin

baby

grandma

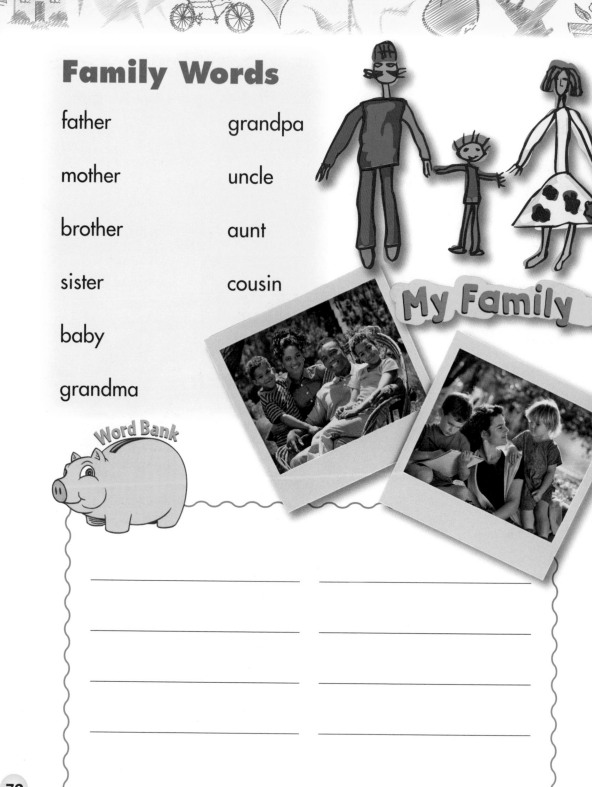

Word Bank

My Family

Feeling Words

hot	tired
cold	excited
happy	angry
sad	silly
scared	sick

angry

happy

sad

excited

Word Bank

Seasons and Weather

spring

summer

fall

winter

rain

snow

clouds

storm

windy

sunny

Word Bank

Today is cloudy.
Where is the sun?

74

Animal Names

lion

lion	hippo
tiger	frog
snake	bird
elephant	mouse
giraffe	bear

frog

Word Bank

Nature Words

beach	mountains
lake	woods
ocean	forest
seashore	flower
desert	stream

flower

desert

Word Bank

mountains

Transportation

travel	road
train	jet
bus	airport
car	ship
taxi	rocket

taxi

bus

jet

Word Bank

My Neighborhood

school	police station
library	hospital
grocery store	office
bakery	park
fire station	playground

playground

park

Word Bank

Food

apple	chicken
banana	pizza
carrots	soup
spaghetti	milk
taco	ice cream

pizza

taco

banana

Word Bank

My Alphabet Word List

Add your own words. Keep a list of favorite words, new words you learn, or difficult words. Use these words in your writing.

Aa

ape

around

away

1. _____

2. _____

3. _____

4. _____

5. _____

6. _____

Bb

bed

below

better

1. _____

2. _____

3. _____

4. _____

5. _____

6. _____

Cc

cake

city

color

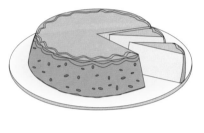

Dd

did

doll

duck

1. _____

2. _____

3. _____

4. _____

5. _____

6. _____

1. _____

2. _____

3. _____

4. _____

5. _____

6. _____

Ee

eagle

easy

energy

Ff

flower

forest

fork

1. _____	1. _____
2. _____	2. _____
3. _____	3. _____
4. _____	4. _____
5. _____	5. _____
6. _____	6. _____

Gg

gate

going

grow

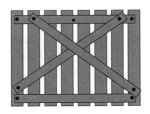

Hh

helper

house

hurt

1. _____

2. _____

3. _____

4. _____

5. _____

6. _____

1. _____

2. _____

3. _____

4. _____

5. _____

6. _____

Ii

ice

igloo

inside

Jj

jeep

jump

just

1. _____

2. _____

3. _____

4. _____

5. _____

6. _____

1. _____

2. _____

3. _____

4. _____

5. _____

6. _____

Kk

kangaroo

kind

know

Ll

lamp

leaf

little

1. _____

2. _____

3. _____

4. _____

5. _____

6. _____

1. _____

2. _____

3. _____

4. _____

5. _____

6. _____

Mm

milk

money

morning

Nn

near

nest

never

1. _____

2. _____

3. _____

4. _____

5. _____

6. _____

1. _____

2. _____

3. _____

4. _____

5. _____

6. _____

Oo

octopus

of

only

Pp

people

pig

please

1. _____

2. _____

3. _____

4. _____

5. _____

6. _____

1. _____

2. _____

3. _____

4. _____

5. _____

6. _____

Qq

quarter

queen

quiet

Rr

read

right

rope

1. _____

2. _____

3. _____

4. _____

5. _____

6. _____

1. _____

2. _____

3. _____

4. _____

5. _____

6. _____

Ss

school

show

sock

Tt

table

their

together

1. _____

2. _____

3. _____

4. _____

5. _____

6. _____

1. _____

2. _____

3. _____

4. _____

5. _____

6. _____

Uu

umbrella

uniform

until

Vv

valentine

van

very

1. _____

2. _____

3. _____

4. _____

5. _____

6. _____

1. _____

2. _____

3. _____

4. _____

5. _____

6. _____

Ww

where

window

would

Xx

excellent

x-ray

xylophone

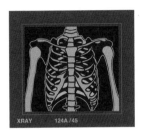

1. _____

2. _____

3. _____

4. _____

5. _____

6. _____

1. _____

2. _____

3. _____

4. _____

5. _____

6. _____

Yy

yarn

yesterday

your

Zz

zebra

zinnia

zipper

1. _____

2. _____

3. _____

4. _____

5. _____

6. _____

1. _____

2. _____

3. _____

4. _____

5. _____

6. _____

My Ideas for Writing

Keep a list of things you want to know more about.
Look at these when you need to write.

_____   _____

_____   _____

_____   _____

_____   _____

_____   _____

_____   _____

_____   _____

_____   _____

Index

Traits of Good Writing Index